ALSO BY ROBERT STEWART

*Working Class*, poems

*The Narrow Gate*, essays

*Plumbers*, poems

*Outside Language*, essays

*On Swerving: The Way of William Stafford,* essay

*Chickenhood*, poetry chapbook

*

ANTHOLOGIES EDITED

*New American Essays* (co-edited)

*Spud Songs: Anthology of Potato Poems* (co-edited)

*Decade: Modern American Poets* (co-edited)

*Voices from the Interior: Missouri Poets*

# Higher

# Higher

POEMS

ROBERT STEWART

THE POETRY PRESS OF PRESS AMERICANA
Los Angeles | Hollywood

Published by
The Poetry Press of Press Americana
americanpopularculture.com



Cover Art: "Vineyard Vista" (detail), oil on canvas, 24 x 24 inches, by Carol Zastoupil, carolzastoupil.com

Cover Design: James Dissette.

Library of Congress Cataloging-in-Publication Data

Names: Stewart, Robert, 1946- author.
Title: Higher / Robert Stewart.
Description: Hollywood, Los Angeles : The Poetry Press of Press Americana, [2023] | Summary: "The poems in Higher are at once direct and resonant, celebratory of the natural world and of spiritual aspirations. The poems rise from a working-class, blue-collar sensibility--from a short poem about using a sledge hammer on a street crew, to a multi-part poem of animals in changing nature. These lyric poems include subtle metrics and enough narrative to drive events, often with elegiac references to a military vet friend, a brother, a Sicilian grandmother, and literary heroes. Their focus ultimately returns to hope and care for children, often with no small amount of humor. These poems from the winner of a National Magazine Award and Prize Americana attest to our ability to pay attention, to detail what we see and what we hear, and, as such, aspire to joy"-- Provided by publisher.
Identifiers: LCCN 2023000987 | ISBN 9781735360164 (paperback)
Subjects: LCGFT: Poetry.
Classification: LCC PS3569.T469 H54 2023 | DDC 811/.54--dc23/eng/20230112
LC record available at https://lccn.loc.gov/2023000987

*FOR* LISA D. STEWART

*O, Once I lov'd a bonnie lass,*
*An' aye I love her still . . .*
—Robert Burns

*&*

*FOR* ROBERT BALICE STEWART
AND MILES JAMES KANE

*Then let us pray that come it may,*
*As come it will for a' that,*
*That Sense and Worth, o're a' the earth*
*Shall bear the gree, and a' that.*
—Robert Burns

Contents

I.



II.

III.

# I.

*What child is this? A very profound question.*
—Marilynne Robinson, "Wondrous Love"

*They're all our children now.*
—David Ray, "Bhopal"

# IN THE BACK PEWS ON EASTER AT ST. ANN'S IN PRAIRIE VILLAGE, & SIMULTANEOUSLY ST. ELIZABETH'S IN WALDO, ST. FRANCES & DOUBTLESS OUR LADY OF SORROWS, MIDTOWN

Babies being carried out to howl
in the lobby, then carried back in,
passing each other, babies with backs
arched in some kind of agony, eyes
scrunched shut, babies beginning
to toddle, who return on their own
tiny feet, picked up, passed back
and forth, moms to dads to grandmas,
who sit with the book for babies,
birds, giraffes, and babies moaning
full-out wails, dropping to the floor
and chased under pews, breaking
crayons, babies banging Tonka trucks,
babies held by friends in the parish,
babies going *guhg, oogh,* teething
a shoulder, waving to the young
man here alone, behind the baby,
waving back, smiling, grandmas
kissing the little fingers after babies
have been on the floor, babies
crawling the aisles for the readings
of Acts and Psalms and the stone
the builders rejected, scooped up
before they topple the little table
with cruets of water and wine,
babies grasping the basket lined
with cash, and everyone holding
babies to their shoulders, during
Colossians and John, laughing
with babies at the Elevation.

## TASKS DONE AND UNDONE

*I pass death with the dying and birth with the new-wash'd babe,*
*and am not contain'd between my hat and boots.*
—Walt Whitman

Better today if I had gone home to work
on the wooden gate, which is coming apart,
but the robin has hatched her brood
on the downspout nearby and stares at me
if I get close or make the gate groan, as in a poem
I read recently with the opening line thus:
Would everybody stop dying, please? Whitman
no longer is contained between hat and boots;
and Roth, this morning announced his silence,
and Pope Francis, himself, says in a movie,
he is not immortal. The Pope. So I repeat,
Don't die, please, and still agree to carry
the casket of my pal Bob, at Jefferson Barracks
National Cemetery, on his way through
the squeaky gate. I am a realist.

## WISHES FOR THE WORLD

I want to be down on my knees,
pulling radishes in the garden, raised

bed or spaded dirt; and if a stranger
comes along, I want to point her way

with a radish, or bunch of mustard greens
already tied with twine and lying

in a basket with tomatoes. I want
to lift the nest lid mornings and trouble

the comfortable, getting pecked,
sure, but that's what I want. I want

brown eggs so fresh the shells
hardly crack on the caste-iron ridge

of the skillet, scramble them
in chopped radishes, greens—

you see all this coming together—
over cool slices of those very tomatoes.

It doesn't sound like much, but
there are so many refugees, I want

also to hold their babies awhile
and let feeling return to their arms,

and I want to say, sometimes
when I was a kid we had nothing
for breakfast but donuts.

## PEOPLE SO HUNGRY

*Look on meat; think it dirt, then eat a bit.*
—George Herbert

Holiday ham or bird appears
at half time, with mud cookies
sunning in Haiti, roof-top
convections for even baking.

I hear this being broadcast—
"A bum came up to me saying,
'I haven't eaten in two days.'"
You know what's coming—

Henny Youngman says to him,
"You should force yourself."
Exclamation marks after each
sentence have been harvested,

like tender, wild asparagus.
Gone. Let each word appear
as it is. No one needs to be told
what eye or ear should desire.

Who wants to say grace?—
a question stomach asks eternity.
*These are Thy gifts. Thy bounty.*
In "The Potato-Eaters," 1885,

the sod cutter wants his scalloped;
the other man requests mashed;
the girl in her billowy dress says
yams with those little marshmallows.

*Take this and eat.* Think of it.
W.C. Fields said the Depression

forced him to live for days on nothing
but food and water. All delivered

in time, as the dew that left
in its place coriander seed, flour
tempered with oil, and tamarisk.
"There are people in the world

so hungry," the Mahatma says,
"God cannot appear to them—"
You know what's coming—
"except in the form of bread."

## SQUEEZED IN

Easter, I make myself space
in a pew facing a pillar
four feet wide, I'd say, gray,
mottled, plastered countenance,

and the woman squeezed
to my left worries I cannot see
the priest or chorus or babies
lined up for a blessing, late

as I am to celebrate
the empty tomb, while kids
here at St. Francis climb
over my knees, in and out

against this stanchion,
as if I were the father, raising
them close among us
who see as best we can.

## THE SCRIPT

Usually, someone gets it,
tracked down or shot,
and someone pauses
at the brink of eternity
after being worked over
by a Johnny Friendly,
and Brando says, "Father,
Get me to my feet"—
meaning, *Keep us alive.*

In her room in our house,
my wife is writing a movie,
without Billy clubs this time,
druggy moms, or winter's
pond hiding a body, and no
dock-worker foreman
to underscore the radical
discontinuity of death,
just me this time, walking
for a brother's funeral,

his cheeks stuffed and hair
combed back like a union
boss. What's at stake?
my wife asks of each draft
she brings to the table.
How could I ask less
of the undertaker's craft—
to *Keep us alive* or fool us
with appearances.

The casket's opening closes
for Dan, 53; no need to ask
what is real, body or image.

My niece touches his hair
as did Eva Marie Saint
for her brother in the film
to save him from himself.
Flashbacks on mortuary
easels document that, yes,
we step into our own punches.

Call it drink this time.
Call it a whistle unheard
at the credits and, finally,
*All right, let's go to work—*
while former associates
stake out the split-level,
2.5 baths—appearing now
in my wife's kind of movie,
where every kid, Dan included,
gets to his feet—and becomes,
yes, a somebody—before
a bozo, a tough, a goon
puts him in a box.

This isn't his day or mine
in the script. Understate
the dialogue for a plot turn,
my wife advises, yet I stand
at Calvary Cemetery, busted up,
a mouse under an eye, and call
to the trees and clouds,
*You want 'im—you can have 'im,*
so even the father knows, Dan
was somebody's brother.

## HOW I STOPPED THE CHICKENS FROM GETTING OUT

I packed duct tape over the hook
and eye the hens pecked at.

While the roll was out, I pressed
a strip over the plantar wart

I suspected on the sole of my foot
and stood on it. I could see

then the horse would not hold
for shoeing so I remembered to hang

a strip of duct tape off his nose
to calm him down.

That did it. Immediately after lunch,
I could walk the road with the dog

whose collar I had studded with duct tape
to keep down fleas, as I read once

on the humor page of *The New Yorker*
thinking it was serious.

The dog and I started to run,
taking my heart for granted,

even if last night my closest sister

appeared in my dream as having died.
If they find a leak in a valve

I tell my wife, duct tape my mouth
silver or gray

for my tendency to embellish a story
and regretting it later.

## THE ENVELOPE

The arrival, bordered black—
news of a death from the old
country—which the boy's
grandmother would leave intact

on her dresser, and would point
to it from her table, and would weep
at first for Anthony, then Maria, then
imagine a child had returned

too soon to heaven, and named
there, in the filmy document.
Her candles grew in number
each time she dreamed of another

inhabitant massed inside those
seams and corners. *We*, our lights,
flickered in her bureau mirror—
child, cousin, brother—the words

on paper unconsumed: no good
news in the folds of someone's last
thoughts while making the sauce,
perhaps, or parking the machine.

*Return to the heart*, said Augustine
bishop of Hippo. In the heart,
you hear where also you can see
all things as one. In this flat,

all-knowing, one-ounce angel
of mourning, costing so, most mail
would go by ship or by the slow,
prop-driven island hoppers, time

had landed in a kind of stall, and all
the present and past appeared
as through a low ceiling or,
as the Lord, right through a wall.

I'll tell you, now. I, the boy,
might have opened the envelope
and had it done, but I had come to love
the sound of cries for everyone.

## VIRTUOUS PIGEONS

They always came back, unless
dead from a hawk or mean kid.
They circled the yard, on leaving,

ever widening around the maple
twins in McCarthy's yard next door,
reappearing over treeless Camarota's

and each time elevating their circle
by perspective and virtue, shrunk
to something you could wear
on a finger; then one of the birds,

but a facet of light now to the eye,
seemed to know where to go,
for Texas or northern Illinois
if it were born there, sparking

fidelity this time to the man
whose birds they once were,
though he'd moved years before

from the loft in south St. Louis,
so his name, too, has feathered,
and my father would drive me

to that empty shed to find inside
the strawberry, blue-banded,
splashed and mottled birds perched
as I'd prayed on a pile of lumber.

## ARRIVALS

> *WHEREAS, feral hogs are currently reported to cause an estimated $800 million per year in damages nationwide . . .*
> —Missouri Governor Matt Blunt

1.

Pigs, *sus scrofa*, push up
their quotas of past millennia.
Out of Arkansas, they remodel
Missouri; they alter Iowa.
Armadillos scale asphalt
in Taney County, squashed
little babies that once waggled
hello-like at the Texas border.
Oh, baby. It's new nature.
Pigs sailed with Columbus
to the West Indies, and with
de Soto to Florida, grubbers
below snow line, in hardwood
and marsh, low to the ground,
unable to thermoregulate
or control themselves at all,
so selling out other pigs works
in targeted areas, to identify
by radio telemetry the swine
in association, the gatherings
of hogs. We shoot them all
except, of course, the Judas.

2.

Ten miles south of the confluence
of the Missouri and the Kaw,
I scoop scraps of lumber and leaves
from an outbuilding whose glazing
failed after twenty years, moving
as I am with heat and wind,
windowpanes dislodged to grass
or shattered on cement paths
with the gnawed, sawed-up sections
of white pillar post from the first
front porch. That crazy poet
Donne, centuries past, called
on God to break, blow, burn,
and make him new; so I know,
standing in this shed, shovel
in hand, piles of rotted wood
nearly to my knees, the possum
that comes startled and terrified
up as from some festering glory
must be the holiest pig of the yard,
prophet of new nature, and I
its associate all along.

3.

Last night, my wife took out
the dog and let him run off
leash, back home. He ran and ran,
and she returned to the house
alone, whistling and clapping
into the long-darkened order
of tires, trees, bagged trash.
She could not sleep for damages
the night might cause, feral hearts
low to the ground, that neither
settle down nor rise and stand.
And yes, the dog returned at dawn
with his usual whining apology,
turning himself in, the accident
that brought him home alive
stored in the scent of memory,
like bubbles in a fish tank—
lenses that wobble up hello.

4.

Now, Zen masters act unlike
themselves—This fly, Basho says,
"See how it wrings its hands."
See how our nephew home
from his war tells us no
stories, sitting in the dark
kitchen, 3 a.m., everyone else's
*scala natura*e eternal, immutable
as macadam, here, at the cross
of the country. Welcome back.
My wife stoops to the fury-
faced mutt Sadie and says,
"You're beautiful, the most
beautiful girl in the world,"
enough to untangle a chain
of being, great or not, so this
creature, too, might migrate
—beauty being peace, some say—
and not to get too far afield,
now the southern leopard frog
shows up on Staten Island,
and those big, watery eyes
seem to insist: Let's see your
movie actress bat these.

5.

Sixty years ago this poem,
the first artificial satellite
took a look over our rivers
and woods, its *beep, beep,*
on newscasts so articulate
we thought it meant, Here
we are, Lord, monitored
like Sister Mark had said,
visible and moving across
state line with mice, minnows,
bloodhounds that find
my socks scattered in circles,
in street view, in hybrid maps
and thistles *beep, beeping*
on the backs of creatures
I cannot know, for I am not
a possum or pig, but with
them in new nature, low
to the ground and grunting.

6.

Talk radio talks of nature
in the city—deer, too many;
falcons leaping from ledges
on the AT&T office tower,
two sparrows worth a farthing,
a mountain lion, confirmed,
finally, when run over by a jeep,
TV news zooming down onto
the cat's huge paws, a synecdoche
for when a part becomes the whole.
I love their lies. The possum
in hell's garden shed did not
scream. The pig, *sus scrofa*,
cast no votes for beauty in its fellows.
They get too close and fleas
bed down with the beautiful,
and even the poet Issa,
really crazy, said, sorry, fleas,
my house is so small.

7.

Let them in. Let the dog,
on the butte of the sofa-back
at the window, look over
the suburban drive, snow
flaking through the meshed
security door—no burglar
look-alikes, zebra mussels
or country-music jamborees
creeping in on today's mail,
across living and dining rooms.
I have found the holiday-tree
disposal lot for renewables,
where the park department parks
its chipper: *No grass clippings*,
yells the sign. No computer parts;
no nonindigenous damages nationwide.
Only this. The Gospel Pig
and the gnosis of its claims: If
*Something there is that doesn't love a wall,*
another crazy poet said—the hams,
the thinning sky—the paradise
our pig has rooted for now is found.

## II.

*To sun, to feast, and to converse*
*and all together—for this I have abandoned*
  *all my other lives.*
—Robert Francis, "Waxwings"

*All things are ready, if our minds be so.*
—*Henry V*, Shakespeare

## HOME EARLY

I come home early  
and get coals going in the grill.  
My wife,  
on the sectional and watching  
*Judge Judy,* has on  
her pained face. She puts the judge  
on mute so a buzz  
continues from the gizzards  
of the TV, as if  
conglomerated by diversified  
or contrary fields.  
*This headache could stand a bull,*  
she says—a horse  
that won't back down. I get the part  
of standing a bull,  
having read Ionesco and want  
the rhinoceros,  
fascist, bloviation out of her head  
forever. *What gives*  
*with those people?* she says.  
They show up to court  
with no documents—nada, zip,  
but grunts and attitude—  
always capitulating and expecting justice.  
She gets to her feet,  
and I—pain free, home early—  
get the rubs out  
for a little line up: Bucktown Brown  
Mustard, Chimayo chili,  
a bottle of tear salt from the sea's  
neurotransmitters,  
all forming a little chorus of *Shout—*  
*A little bit softer, now,*

my fingers fretting the hollow,
        base of her skull,
and I think it helps—no flashes
        or retinal flakes,
no floats, no spinning prairie sun
        or curtain closing
on the periphery, just, *Go out*
        *and turn the meat,*
she says, so I do the right thing
        for once. The coals
have formed a chimney of smoke
        to climb out of.

## MY FATHER'S HAUNT

*(St. Louis, north side.)*

As at the tavern by a mountain stream
in a poem by Ho Xuan Huong,
Whalen's Bar has hot dogs and chili
in the back room, whoops like owls
in the bamboo, and NFL Rams
burning carbs on the big screen.

I stop in, my pickup's tailgate
backed to the front window, and ask
what's on tap? *You aren't from here*,
someone yells, among keg-like
shapes at the center table: Polish,
German, Italian, black and Irish.

There's a picture of men in overalls
with folding rules in their leg pockets,
and I imagine the plumb line
dropping from the upper floors
of a world they built. *I am from here.*
Work is work; beer's a beer.

I pincer out a hot dog from
rust-colored cooker water and wattle
its neck loose of what could be
dew or acid rain, in the faded glow.
I like these guys and know them,
and the bar maid, whose *Busch, Busch Light*

seems to answer all questions, even mine.
*Where is my father?* We'd call this place
and hear, tossed around in the hands
of buddies, like a fish hard to catch,
our own last name, *Stewart*, laboring
in valleys of imagination, being served.

## YELLOW FLOWER

When one appeared on the power line,
*drink your tea* it seemed to say

like a goldfinch. Wind took
its wavy pattern of flap twice

and tuck, soar and swoop,
nothing new to the winds of Kansas.

Even dandelions and camphorweed
flock to us this time of year.

## THE SLEDGE

We always had a sledge
in my father's garage—
a sixteen-pound, long handle
wrapped at the neck
in black, fabric tape
for a fender. Around
that tape I wrapped
my left hand, holding
the sledge waist high
before swinging
from the end with both
hands, arms extended,
to break bricks, flatten
buckets, fix a wheel.
I would drive horseshoe
pegs and tent stakes
for when neighbors
gathered in our yard.
When I had grown
enough to use a sledge
on a street crew, I broke
the handle once right
where tape had wrapped
my father's sledge,
when the 16-pound
head overstruck its mark.
The foreman told
another man on the crew
to take over, handed
him a fresh sledge,
but I took it from him.
Both men just looked

at me and stood back—
I never have forgotten—
while I swung again
on concrete from high
above my head.

## KANSAS: ARS POETICA

Wind off the prairie makes me want to punch
back at something. It elbows the windows
and nearly killed my dog, Sparky, cracking
a limb off the lady next door's dead elm
I could barely drag off the drive, dents
in the F-150 but just the bed. Wind
swings the big wooden gate, so lets out
the dog and has the wood fence leaning
northeast, and the phone wire, dragging
a cord off a cello all night, getting
into our business. It's a summer wind
but not like the Sinatra song, from the sea.
It sucker punches into car windows,
so walking along 75th can kill you, Frank.
All summer long, we sing our song,
my wife and I, if cobwebs we call cable
and power grids don't crash our computers
for once. My wife drives her nails into
my T-shirt in the yard, holding on.
"You're too big to make a dent in," she says.
A prevailing wail corners the house
and makes me want to take on the beater of time.
A cottonwood seed courses over crops
like a comet. A boxwood leaf karate chops.
No lingering in pools that stand in drains:
rotations, convections, sideways rains.
Someone has opened a job box
of westerly wind and has us leaning,
as we'd been taught, which is into it.

## THE NOTE,

*—ending with a line by James Tate*

the sound of an empty
beer bottle hitting
a freshly mowed lawn,

lobbed through silence
of proscribed
duration, about ten feet

maybe three, four
seconds, though Tate
once said it took him

three hours to get
to a jumping-off place,
and like him, the bottle

made a hollow-headed
note, hitting
ground, as if blown

through cupped palms,
whistle-like, a coo
for mourning, a *Bonk*—

the arrival of an idea,
say, at a place
anyone could rest

and not shatter,
sweat still sipping
at your forehead

and the sky pinned
like the pages of a book
written by a dove.

## WHERE I WAS THEN

Where did I see those turkeys?
In a dream? No, flightless
as a dream, I saw the turkeys
out by Longview Lake Sunday
as I was driving to make Mass
at 10:30, where I expected
the priest to apologize to us all.

He had not fired the lesbian
food-pantry manager but had
stood for the bishop to do it.
Those wild, Missouri turkeys
don't flutter easily like doves
but stand in shadow between
the road and the tree line.

I am tempted to call the turkeys
clerics in their dark cassocks,
but that figure, too, must wait
for when I am fully awake
and the upright birds rise,
as if born from shadows
just beyond the shelterbelt.

# LIGHTS OUT

Now we consumers—colleagues
of corporeality, say—have filled
our humongous carts with a cache

of cabernet, cheeses, Poise Pads,
and Ensure for elderly relatives,
the drift of constellation Costco,

so much product I could send
you readers a pallet full of paper plates,
and then, given end times predicated

by profligacy and base pandering—
as if there were any other pandering—
lights go out, and, amazement to all,

go slowly out, like an easeful landing
of the Otis elevator that had dropped us
from Chicago's observation

of the metropolis, slowing, surely
as the overheard, dying breath
of a beloved basset hound, and down,

down to darkness—darkness, I discovered
beside the batches of blueberries—
attached to a buzzer so loud

a man in a white, button-down shirt
asks me—*me*—What's going on?
(or *What's going down?*). Don't know:

my starless, airless answer. Unsaid,
I thought the near-scream of alarm
and darkness so obviously connected,

so true to my preparatory education,
that the man asking might have been
Dante in the City of Woe, listening

in tears—"the near-deafening chorus
of a million dolls' dark inner voices"—
all our material desires indigesting

the Great American Chocolate Cake
of fortunate darkness—*fortunate*,
says a lecture-woman described

in email circulars as the Comedienne
of Near-Death Experience, who
once met her own loud, near-end

when a strange man, perhaps in white,
button-down shirt, swept her off
the sidewalk where she had dropped

into peace and love of brilliant,
golden light. I'm pulled by this string
of adjectives out from the maze

I had led myself into, the joke
of knowing death is nothing we need
to own, even as I am signing up

for the light, which returns now,
like stars at the end of the journey—
hardly a punch line—but I am

at last learning to let go, let go
one case of frozen shrimp, one
bundle of bath towels at a time.

## STANDING

*I will spare the whole place for their sake.*
—Genesis 18

Those teenage boys stand
against the back wall
for Mass at Little Flower,

heads bowed, fingers
running rosaries and soft
fists striking their chests,

Sunday duty done
inside the outer door
of the circular corridor,

backs pressed to stone,
some resting on one leg,
as if in stride to clear

a hurdle or lift up
our hearts. *Lord,*
they say, *I am not worthy.*

How can they believe
anything but the touch
of immortality, robed

in cargo shorts or jeans.
*Only say the word*, I know
they dutifully repeat,

walking their hosannas
into the altar dome's
light born over and over,

so we get a good look
at them, bare heads
and huge, white sneakers,

sparing us a moment
concern for our souls
and all this talk of eternity.

## PIRANHA, CHRISTMAS DAY

*from everything a little always remains*
—Carlos Drummond de Andrade

The people of Rosario
wade, biblically almost,

into the river filled with,
if not named for, eaters

of the flesh. Rio Paraná
alludes to *big as the sea,*

through Brazil, Paraguay,
Argentina, where I am

to believe no one
had a sign, only faith.

Easter, flesh to spirit goes,
while the day of birth,

spirit takes flesh and blood,
as in: This is thy flesh.

Eat of it. This thy blood,
fingers and toes. Take them

and eat. Who was I, then,
coursing down current

in a dugout on the headwaters
of The Paraná, passport

taken by soldiers and thrown
like a pack of matches

into a desk drawer
by an open window.

*It will be here when you return, señor,*
—and was—turning me

into a creature of faith. Signs,
maps, local wisdom, the sense

I was born with suggested
I would not return but continue

southeast into blood sprayed
at Iguazu Falls, the torrent

of a continent, Rio de la Plata,
the Atlantic, to find what? Sharks.

A little always remains at the mouth
of rivers, wrote Carlos Andrade.

Though a man on shore says,
"I warn you against it," and a student

says, "It is a fish gone crazy,"
the swimmers of Rosario, Argentina,

return one hour after the attack,
suspended in their water

big as the sea, its name that
sounds like *piranha.*

## WHERE FENCES FORM THE ROAD

*Desultory*, a word you know yet
don't, when the woman riding along
and reading Thomas Hardy from your
college, quality-paperback Borzoi,
with its original price fading $1.35,
says, Well, you already know if Tess
recovers here; and you say look
at the price and tell me how long
you think it's been since I read that.

She pulls up one of a two-volume
dictionary off the floorboard, her peach
fingernail *des, des, des'es* down the page
and stops. *Leaping about*, living
by chance, anything but steady,
she says, something every novel
needs, but what of us? This family

visit you'd like the world as it was,
the sum of the surname spun
to its constituency; but you know
not to bundle the past, maybe just
sing your Lou Rawls "At Last"
and not ask, Who are we?—
Hardy's question in the novel
you won't admit to remembering,
won't stop bringing to the surface.

All turns out fine, you say. An angel
at an angle to the sun appears
as a deer and, as a deer, vanishes
by leaping the cyclone fence
into only a word for itself, a *hart*,
given deer, deer, deer in the field.

Imagine you found your family
like this, against a side-yard fence
in a city the old French elegantly
named for a king and saint, its red
brick homes, ash pits, and alleys
and your beautiful sister's arms
bruised by intravenous bumbling,
propped by pillows in a lawn chair.

Your future wife slows you down
to read the scene you know yet
don't, the schisms and abdications
that come in names no one dates
or defines at the porcelain table
of past glory. You scan the list
of present terms for what love—
Oh, sing it now—"has come along."
Your sister's husband yells, happy
to see her smiling. Wouldn't you
ask cousins, kids and friends here
to join you in leaping about—
leaping, leaping the damn fences?

## GIARDINIERA

*for Lis*

I knew what she was doing,
my wife, in this gathering to include
a serrano pepper, our youngest
produce, an onion, and clove
of garlic, soaking in salt water

like biology class, so intent is she
to know even the chemistry
of a burp. Chop cauliflower,
carrots, all evening the chatter
of knife on board like little waves

clapping on the hull of the boat
in the tub. Forget about the order
seasonings call from across the sea.
I know what she sees; inside a jar,
the garden all accounted for—

is this why we marry, halfway
through a life? Children beget
and get begotten, and on we relish
the Italian in us, content to
embellish with pepper and squash.

## RUNNER, PAUSING, ALONE

A woman massages her legs, maybe
restarts a jog along the logging road,
having glimpsed gray muzzles, heard
gravel crack, and must have known,
then, the only carnivores active
in the area have her going lame.
*Brother wolf, you do much harm,*
St. Francis would admonish, hunger
or not, and no Tiber River nearby
to carry her away. Alaskan tall scrub
fourteen meters off road would hide
the body, thirty-two years old, described
as small and mighty, everything
required for the soul's recourse.

How can we not laugh at ourselves
for saying, *The wolves are at our heals*
when a mountain of bills becomes
a mountain without pine trees,
or call *Luxury the wolf at the door,*
as Tennessee Williams once said?
*A patient wolf,* Lana Turner defined
a gentleman, taking us to wit's end
on the logging road, days later when
a man of the village council arrives
by snowmobile. Tracks all around
the body, he says, choosing words
carefully, and drag marks associated
with those tracks. Wolf involvement?
*It's obvious. Goodness. It's obvious.*
He did not want to elaborate.

## ACCOUNT FOR THIS

*for Willis Barnstone*

An account comes two days later
when the daughter on social media
says he was giving a talk at Harvard
Divinity—the divine, I imagine
always present, though he giving
the talk had written, "no sad /
faces, no body or sick word of God,"
capitalizing yet the name,
leaving us to wonder of both He
and he, author and translator
of the Testament Restored, giving
the talk at Divinity, when he lost
sight in one eye, "And then,"
the daughter says, "it came back.
(He read most of the talk with one eye),"
and no one could account for that
or get him to Tufts for a check-up,
even the next day when half light
struck again at a museum—
this being Cambridge, after all—
with Rossetti's "The Blessed Damozel"
and Sullivan's "Canyon de Chelle,"
secular enough for single sight until
one understands the ever-present
stones and flowers, the present
feeling that comes to those we love,
father, friend, though getting him
to ER's machines and needles
would take the daughter, her brother,
and one whose voice I do not know,
a certain mystery that won't account
for limitations of the body, or admit
to less than he of whom we speak.

## OUR HAPPINESS

Do you remember our happiness
when the electricity came back?
Lights forgotten those days
of cold, heavy dark, sprung on
like a dog startled by a latch.
The refrigerator began to whine
as from the rubble of a disaster,
its food all gone—milk,
bacon, leftover linguini. So long
were we without cheese,
I had forgotten grapes,
crackers, roasted garlic,
and gritty, sharp Romano
with claret. Without
the balm of furnace breezes
billowing from vents
I had forgotten desire,
reds and bourbons.
We walked through the house
like members of the James gang
who hid out in caverns in bluffs
along the Meramec, and maybe
wondered if they might have gone
another direction, worked
the dirt, or iron, or split logs,
as we, ourselves, would stop
now and then to wonder
about the TV in the window
across the road, blinking
its blue light from centuries
in the future, how it seemed
to promise another life
that one day would flicker
for disbelievers and us, alike,

and I would say, Oh, Honey,
let us restock the fridge,
and you would say, Oh, Love,
we have all that we need.

## DOG IN CHURCH

I'm a boy standing in his church
again, waiting for a nun
to orbit the altar.

So used am I to this round
church, by adulthood
the nave aisle of St. Mary

Magdalen on Manchester,
or College Church on Grand—
any architectural world

with end, straight shot
for the monstrance—
appeared pedestrian, until

that is, I walked with my son
one August into Basilica
Santa Croce, Florence,

where we cooled off
beside the grave of Galileo,
which gives rise to this moon

of a nun circling the sacristy,
Church of the Little Flower,
where I spent nine school years

I want to tell Sister—Sister,
eyeballing a small dog
she turns out to be chasing;

and there, by the life-sized
agony of Mary, it goes
for my shins, a pug, I think—

anti-matter, space junk—
no bishop would condemn
my booting to a separate path

if the laws of heaven,
like the chain of being,
have no bearing anymore.

Sister arrives to proclaim,
"It's Father's dog," patrolling
its world freely as a Doge.

How is it Galileo can invent
the universe, and I am
here with a dog in church

and a nun raising a ring
of keys to point my way
toward the door with a key?

Yes, Sister. I came back
to this church because
I did not want to grow up.

The kneeler. Rail. Slap
on the face when the bishop
confirmed us *Domini Canes,*

hounds of the Lord,
lead me elliptically
around these grounds

again, where dogwoods
lay white clusters of petals
on their outer circles.

## DIGGING SPARKY'S GRAVE

*I dreamt the past was never past redeeming.*
—Richard Wilbur

I make a bigger production of it
than necessary. I get a spade
from the shed, and a round point,
a square point, and an axe. Lay
a four-by-eight-foot sheet of 3/8th-inch
plywood in the grass by the location;
I will need the wheelbarrow
from the shed for excess dirt.
A lot more comes out of a hole
than goes back in. Then, there's the dog.

Laborers I worked with years ago
on the sewer crew would score
the grass to shape the hole
before taking a cut, a production
to signal the gracious going down
of work and time. I score a rectangle
the size of a medium dog house,
squaring the sides with the spade
and crumbing with the round point
like I was taught, to make a ditch

clean. Two feet down, a root
off the elm jolts me spade to hip,
a breath caught. I haven't used a shovel
in five years but to bury a squirrel
or rabbit the dog caught and shook
and tried to hide from me.
Our yard offers no exile distant
enough from that tree, and here,
I separate dirt from root, straddle
the hole and short-swing the axe,

missing once, then dissolve the obstacle
and impressions of the task at hand.

He was a sensible dog. He could handle
himself around pickups and horses
and would find his way home from a run.
He almost could emerge here,
unobtrusively, where the dirt pile
rises on the plywood, and pee on it.
I never had him fixed; because he never
changed, his pee was his word
etched on the shed, the deck edge,
the vertical periphery, post or bush,
where he'd hop around on three legs,
then switch directions to cover all doubt
and trespass. He always seemed to make
a bigger production of it than necessary.

# III.

*Some are in bed-sheets, some are in blouses,*
*Some are in smocks: but truly there they are.*

—Richard Wilbur, "Love Calls Us to the Things of This World"

## CHICKENS KNOWN AND UNKNOWN

I loved Chickenman, ca 1966 ff., of Midland City,
I took for St. Louis, then,
on my '50 Ford radio, trumpeting triumphantly,
*Buck, buck, buuuuuuk. Chicken-mannn,*
as he rushed off in his Chicken Coupe
to rescue the still-single Sayde, or to
his human job, selling shoes in the city of shoes—
first in booze, first in shoes (last
in the American League)—fantastic fowl
of footwear—*He's everywhere. He's everywhere*—
even over *Armed Forces Radio*, should
the draft board send me to Fort Leonard Wood.

I loved the San Diego Chicken, ca 1974 ff.,
droopy lids and huge beak—
give me a break—a greater physical comic
I rarely have seen, maybe Danny Kaye,
but the Padres got us all through the fall,
as we used to say, of Vietnam,
as the Chicken appeared with Chuck Berry,
Jimmy Buffett, Paul McCartney, then covered
"Do you think I'm sexy?" by another Stewart
on WIL radio, Cardinals fan or not.

I never loved chasing chickens, or the chicken
chasing my three-year-old sister Christine
with its head cut off, spurting blood,
or the smell of boiling water poured
for plucking pin feathers, and never, ever
loved Henny Penny—too chicken—
or maybe just me, in my soul,
Huey helicopters hovering over the trees

on Kingshighway and Florissant Road,
dropping a big hook for the delta,
where my buddies hung in the sky, ca 1968 ff.,
by the neck, like rubber chickens.

## MY TIME

Anything my people knew
of James Baldwin, May 17, 1963,
*Time* held out on newsstands,
The Negro's Push for Equality,
a necessity to remain calm,

as when McNamara wrote
in *Reader's Digest* why I should
fight in Vietnam. I had failed
five hours of integrated algebra
and trigonometry, first year

of college, on probation by
February 1965, but stayed calm
on Monday, when Malcolm X
took two barrels at the Audubon.
April 1968, I drove supplies

for Sheehan Plumbing on Delmar
in St. Louis; on Friday after
the Memphis shooting (that shooting)
helped young Joe, the owner,
sweep glass from every shop window.

By June, about to leave for active duty,
drove Sheehan's pickup without air
or radio to a job at City Hospital,
plumber in the alley, waiting.
I checked my bill of lading—
toilet bowl, lead cakes, box of oakum.

What could we say? By Thursday,
Kennedy, *that Bobby*,
just had died of wounds in L.A.

Dec. 1, 1987, unions—even the one
my father ran—said the president, *that Reagan*,

needed to decline. I told my son
on Tuesday, age 7, we have our rights.
Baldwin, as it happens, in
Saint-Paul de Vence, France,
just had died. I took it all in stride.

## GUIDE TO THE OUTER ISLANDS

That night along North Lindbergh
years back, by then Sunday morning,
leaving the beer joint and laying myself
out to view stars from the empty
passing lane, Bob, my absolute sidekick,
had time to drag my body back to the gravel
lot, big as I was compared to him.
This was after the redhead drove off,
leaving a scrap of paper with a number
but driving off, nonetheless; Bud neon
flickered in the window and popped
to black. *You always go for the redheads*,
Bob said, as if he knew, as should I, desire
for red hair leads nowhere. The Red Queen,
herself, said it takes all the running you can do
to stay in one place. In mid Lindbergh,
facing up and spread eagle, one could fly
to the outer islands, their houses
roofed with grass, to hunt and eat whales
and wind-dried fish from the blessed sea.
*The dark-haired one really liked you*,
Bob would say, friend and counselor,
knowing red heads were impossible to me
in a neighborhood of dark, Sicilian girls;
but among the tables, smoke, and ashes,
arms swinging as the night turned late,
there seemed to appear some signal fire,
a hyacinthine flower of the Faeroes or Finland –
a boreal copper sky swirling among bands
of light in the juke, filling the jar on the bar
with the pale-blue eggs of a gannet, perhaps
like the blouse of Mary. Forgive me, you girls
and cousins of Italy; so skinny were you
in your short, black, Gina Lollobrigida hair,

I didn't know your beauty or how you loved me.
I wanted to turn toward the sky, myself;
and Bob would say to me, *Hair that red*
*isn't even real*, nor, I knew, was the spark
ignited at their phony ends, good friend
and only purveyor of truth. *So what?*
he'd say. So off she drove in the top-down
Karmann Ghia, the little bottle rocket
of her hair on North Lindbergh going dark
and refiring at each light standard, as far,
at least, as the Shell at Charbonier.

## GANJGAL VALLEY

(*Afghanistan*)

It's a wonder. Our country's newest
winner of the medal of honor steadies
himself on coast-to-coast TV, knew

he would die, he says, a bullet flash
would open his face; while his buddy
Rodriguez-Chavez drove the unarmored

pickup, he, Meyer, Kentucky farm boy,
stood in back with machine gun
on the cab roof, rocking his body,

bullets like static in the air, kind of
cat purr, with all lives issued
and recalled, and get this, the two

went back through that valley
five-damn-times, picking up
co-workers in a car pool, dragging

them home to their wives, blood
covered, dead, even; and let me hear
someone say, now, the boss *ripped you*

*a new one* today, or sent some email,
maybe, you took as offense,
how if you don't die trying, don't know

you will die, Mr. I hate my f-ing job,
you have a few more trips
through the valley, now, don't you?

# A DYING FRIEND CALLS WHILE I AM READING MANUSCRIPTS OF POEMS AT THE MAGAZINE

*—for Ralph*

Then I say, Okay, Buddy, talk
soon but know probably never;
and the stack of paper-clipped
poems has its own bent wings—

a moth pressed in a book—
who could resist the image?
Waxwings sing, again,
in another poem, illusions

to Daedalus and even Eros;
and I realize how unlucky
these fine poets happen to be
when the voice wrapping

things up calls to wish me
happy birthday, wheezingly,
I could say, like a songbird,
but say instead an ex-marine,

a farm boy gone off to gamble
in cards and lose his business,
then work out the debts alone,
toughened and ready, now,

for beauty or truth about
to turn over. Now, this page
at bottom alerts STANZA CHANGE,
otherwise, how would we know?

And really, the poem's good
but has such measure against it
as, *My brother and wife have stayed
all week. Everything's in order.*

## LINEATION

*God, guard me from those thoughts.*
—W. B. Yeats

Don't greet an old man,
*Hello, young man.* Don't
call teammates after
a loss, *winners.* False-
hoods are fine for food
your Maeve, *still young*
*as ever,* fixed, but don't say
to a young man, *I can still*
*kick your sorry ass.* Don't.
Really. It hurts too much.

## POSSUM, UPON THE BACK FENCE,

hog-like and hairy,
razorback without tusks,
head turned like a Greek
wrestler caught in marble
and a flashlight's beam,
dog below like a pillar
in a sandstorm, night
before judgement day
with any action wrong,
justice missing mercy
this moment, dazed
as Demeter's daughter
pulled down among
howls, hoots, hymns
to the corpus, coiled
cougar or snake ingesting
a day-old calf, all wait
and no waddle, not
ignorant, knowing any
act would be its last,
dissembler called
to account for itself
like a stalker on fours
feigning truth between
earth and heaven's sky,
while the dog's tied
to a beast that won't run
and close as all creation.

## NAMES OF THE WIVES

*I'm draggin' the audience to hell with me.*
—Jerry Lee Lewis

We can't say Jerry Lee killed Shawn
Stephens, his second wife, as accused,
or Jaren Elizabeth Gunn Pate, drowned
in a friend's pool, near divorce;

he mourned them in the white suit
and red-ruffled shirt he wore to their
weds, and later, the Ferriday Fireball
bawled at the commotion he spread:

"I plumb married the girl, didn't I?"
meaning not Jaren or Shawn but Myra,
13, his kin. Again, we know the man
from tats and "Life is a Killer" T-shirts.

* * *

Joan Vollmer managed but common
law to William S. Burroughs, a.k.a.
William Tell, her whiskey glass
propped as on a pedestal—the head

of the "wife" shattered for art.
"I am forced to the appalling conclusion,"
said the Godfather of Punk, the Guru
of Get-Gritty, "but for Joan's death,
I never would have become a writer."

* * *

Her place in art. So we sit at a café
with a bugger, drunkard, Sodomite—
each looking fit, and wind cracking
the jib of the patio umbrella—keeping

an eye on us. The actress who played
Killegrew's Desdemona in 1660 goes on
anon., the girl of the family written off,
then Margaret Hughes, Maggie Smith,
Uta Hagen, Claire Danes, smothered

each in turn, each time married in.
Around the horseshoe bar Friday night,
at Romanelli Grille, or O'Dowd's, each
woman turns to say, Him? That bum?
Think of all the wife killers I have known.

* * *

My brother, late one night in Memphis,
steadied his hand on a peaceful shot
of Scotch, when Jerry Lee, the Killer,
the man himself, sat down at the table.
My brother thought nothing of it—

every scream and sob rolled up like smokes
in a shirt sleeve, or inscribed in rings.
"I ain't talkin'," he said, and bought a round.
I can't get closer to the names than recall
how children believe it possible to drown

in a glass of water; sidekick to Othello,
the year we all came alive, I walked
up to William Lee, El Hombre Invisible,
Burroughs, the Elvis of American Letters;
call him the Cosmonaut of Inner Space—

* * *

Sir, I said, would you sign this book?
Would you, Mr. Dillinger, Mr. William B.,
sign my name to a song or story, no one
obscure and known only as the Moor, in dark
corners of wood-frame homes—daughters

and nieces a-wander in the state's last canto?
Tell how we stopped by unannounced,
rang the bell and sat on that porch in Kansas,
you accidently calling me *Cassio.* Who?
I said, and you said, O fool, fool, fool.

## THEY SHOT GOVERNOR GEORGE

*They shot Governor George—*
my buddy and boss at the time
Kent blasted news the year
in St. Louis I drove for his
and Bob's Auto Parts, Monday's
rounds of MasterPro pulleys,
and Gates belts, Monroe shocks,
aluminized-steel, custom shaped
exhaust and tail pipes, tangled
with clutch plates and manifolds
done;
          so it must have been
late p.m., as news traveled,
when *they*, exactly, *they* kept
going down and *they* kept
shooting, and Governor
segregation-forever George,
if I recall, always said he'd go
down like that Kennedy,
Bobby, but seemed conscious
except
          how I surprised myself,
fresh from the Navy, married
and working only for friends—
I mean, only for *having* friends—
the distinction might explain
why the shooting of this poor
blinded, short-legged bastard,
abuser of little girls and boys,
positioned like King Tut on
behalf of traditional privilege,
had me
          pounding a fist
to the hood of the Hazelwood

Auto Parts horse of a pickup
for the governor, an ass
of Tutan slight build we all
believed accounted for some
meanness, and understood
it too well, at heart, each time
Kent gargled out what his brain
seemed trying to fix or repair,
how it could be anyone now
*They shot Governor George.*

## THE GREAT DRYING OFF OF THE WOMEN

*(Poetry Day 2006, Denmark)*

*—for Thomas E. Kennedy*

We got soaked Copenhagen way,
at the Frederiksberg Garden, a Sunday,
scads of Scandinavian poets
with frikadellers for snacks
and a snag in their trouser backs
from the vodka, I think, Stoli,
equally wet; we shouted
among the water courses,
trumpeted in groves and glades,
in the innocent camaraderie
of perhaps a thousand—no
exaggeration—Danish moms and babes
in strollers loosely tarped
so the tots could see verse
carolers standing like herons—no,
they were herons, beaking
the low clouds of August, and one,
reciting squeakily near the "pacifier tree"
where all those kids in strollers
will someday hang up their binkies
with a note like this from a little Alex:
*Here are almost all my pacifiers* (His opening
syntax the model of order).
*I only keep my night pacifier* (now, disorder)
*for a little while yet. Loving regards.*
The little Lear, standing-for
and standing-against, in no-
regret acknowledgment of love,
had strung up all—or mostly all—
his sucking and mumbling devices.

What a man. Out Copenhagen way,
Frederiksberg, our words ran
sonorous and dense as water
rushing off walls and the backs of swans.
Men and women equally, including me,
in my gray, billed cap and wool, poetry-day
blanket crawled to our posts
like crawdaddies to recite our lines.
For a short while, I was miserable
(a predictable syntax) in the rain
and then deliriously happy
with Kennedy at my side, screaming,
"What is it most you want me not to say?"
and off a ways, Neils and Lotte,
Lennox and Gorm, Erik and Marianne
shouting their lines; even the base
of the statue of Frederik VI
had something to say
of his sad childhood and tough life.
Our purple, poetry-day umbrellas,
buoyant as beer caps, bobbed in the green.
What could I do with my curling
pages and sodden underwear but speak
well for the people of our time?
Let the eighteenth century fend for itself.
"I think I can still name my friends dead
of mortar fire," I yelled
out toward Helsingor Strait,
"half a world and full century away."
Oh, you birds, remember that.
Your dazzle in the gray sky
did not empty us. A rivulet of poets
began to move toward the dry
and ancient lobby of a theater
near the *have*—whose name no
longer rises on the bread crumbs

of my brain, though puddles
had all those hungry ducks—
into the bar and audience area,
where the women smelled like waterfalls
and were drying their hair
with paper towels and squeezing
their hems, and kicking off
their sneakers and baring their feet;
birds in the gilded ceiling
or peeking through stained glass
circled them, fanning their bodies
with sunlight. I remember
there was Kennedy, Lisa, Lene,
and Alice, too, with friends from the bar,
and having traveled
(with Lisa) the farthest for this
simple test of adulthood—
to come in out of the rain—I decreed
in a way to be heard at the footlights
that time has come for the drying off
of the women. And the women,
being Danish and American, mostly,
and altogether fit and generous forgave
me immediately, as I knew they would,
which might even have redeemed
the poor, sad life of Frederik the VI—
but why mention him after all this time,
with his autocratic tendencies?
We had our beets and sausages
for dinner later,
and a featherbed for sleep,
as did the Danish moms and babies
for whom a little rain
is a little lyric; and the rain
that soaked us, men and women, alike,
out Copenhagen way,

revealed how close we come
at times to each other's
bodies, the earthly goodness
of our skin, and someone
needed just then
to speak up
about it.

## NEW & SELECTED: POEMS

*—for Sherod Santos*

The selected parts shatter me
every time. The poem sequence
on a man's sister's suicide
has been selected from a book
now ten years old; add
to that the year or two it took
him to write the series, plus
another year for an official
publication date, proofs, &
registration with the Library,
assuming the poet was not,
like most of us, rejected
by dozens of presses first,
year after year, while verses
of his dear sister's world
aged in a drawer or hard drive,
where the mother in her voice
on the phone in section #7
continued to insist, *impatiently*,
"She just died, that's all";
and I am back there, now,
impatient, grieving in the same
guarded way, and can't help
but add up how many years
must pass in the lifespan
of intense emotion, the feeling
that comes first; and naturally,
I wonder what's New, here,
in the book's last section—
if "Life Study with Two Endings"
and its *unloosed, unwashed hair*
alludes to the sister years ago,

as she stripped varnish
from a kitchen table, while
her two daughters napped
beside her on a folded towel.

## FATS

There are good fats and bad fats—
I'm talking to you, Fats, the skinny
guy on stage with a sax, thicker
than your own leg, a leg that's

a shred of bone and gabardine
slacks. All solos take some greed
for sound and "ain't got no Mama now,"
by Harmonica Fats. "I got no need,

no Mama, not now." All that aside,
you're Fats, whether narrow or wide,
whether Waller, doing *the stride*,
or a Creole, Cajun, gastronomical

survival guide. Listen to Domino:
"The Fat Man" didn't mention food,
Dashiell Hammett's Nick and Nora,
either, or what tune Pat Boone

made off with, ain't that a shame.
It's in the name. Saturated or trans,
mono or poly, sound stores up
where the body has its need.

We get our fats from a reed.

## WE HAVE OUR COATS ON

We have our coats on.
Don't the women see us?

The performance has ended.
Our coats are on.

Lobby lights have dimmed,
prosciutto rolls sealed in tubs.

Gas could be turned off
in North America.

Don't they see us,
sitting on the stairs

across from the door
with our coats on?

Perhaps we seem *serene,*
*with our eyes, our shoes, our coats.*

We sit here lined in fleece
dreaming of Bayfield, Wisconsin,

in summer, in T-shirts.
Ten-weight thickens outside

in crank cases, while
the women etch one more

*Best wishes* onto one more
title page. Our coats are

zipped. Our hats are on.
Don't the women see us?

## HIS HEAD

*—for James Tate*

Tell me what happened to his head,
how it rides in neither light nor dark
but keeps bobbing on the ripples

his shoulders have become, the little
farm pond of his chest still stocked;
and the doctor says, look, there's

another fish feeding on dragonflies,
that sort of thing. Pull in the line.
Not long ago, his leg not his head

got restless, kicking over a village
too close to his property line;
no one blamed his head that time,

just his leg syndrome—and who
among us doesn't get that?
Ask the Finns, who have national

standards for kicking things over:
wobbly, as the poles of the earth.
My man was a Finn once, even twice,

before returning to see his mother
in the American suburb outside
his old town, Kansas City. He called

me after three days to say his head
was feeling *blah*, that exact word:
Everything is off white, he said,

demanding of me a favor; he said,
*Get me the hell out of here.* Maybe
he is yelling inside his head, now,

for the same favor. He talks slowly,
so most people get bored at about
the third word. He has written

hundreds of letters to his daughter,
whom he procreated in his former
head; but her husband, the prince,

keeps her locked in a tower and
whips her if she starts dreaming.
My friend says, *I am only the father.*

He scatters birdseed on the surface
of the water, and the fish swim up
as though his brain were a trail

they could follow like the old days,
and it would lead somewhere.

— *New York, 2008*

## STOPPING IN THE ROAD
## FOR A TURTLE

Don't hiss at me. Andre Dubus
rescued that brother and sister
on a highway in Haverville, so let me
here on 55th Street in Crestwood,
6:20 a.m., stop and help you over
to the shrubs.
                    Box turtles I had
as a kid seemed mostly interior,
but you—neck out, jaw wrenching
for my index finger, throat clearing
like an opera singer's—have less
turtleness
                    than serpent;
how heroic of us both, then,
with the pace of such progress,
to trust the car-full universe, when all
Andre Dubus meant to do was act
according to his nature, tough guy.
                    It crippled him
on that road, father of many
characters, and each always seemed
stranded outside a bar, or even home,
listening to some grieving soprano
on the radio. Sing, then turtle, hiss
                    your given voice.

## THE DAY MARIAN ANDERSON SINGS "MY COUNTRY TIS OF THEE"

It is 6:20 p.m., my wife and I have finished dinner,
          shrimp on rice for her, and for me nothing
special, but the dishes are mine, as usual, drying, now,
          on a pad made by Martha Stewart Inc.

As usual, we watch cable news in hopes
          of something hopeful. Yes, a pandemic
and vials of Pfizer iced in Michigan, and my wife
          asks, How many times can we see needle jabs?
and hear the words *into our arms*—if I hear that again—

* * *

so I mute the news and say, Let's read this poem
          here on the coffee table, something called
"At the Thursday Night Jam, Remembering an Absent Singer,"
          where the poet, Henry Taylor—

I'm supposed to say "the speaker," I guess—
          remembers a song his dead pal
used to sing, which Taylor, I mean the speaker, says—
          "It's hard to hear in any voice but his."

We nearly drop dead at that line, so we flip out
          of cable news, entirely, all of its speculating
on what and how and if this, and somehow,
          for once it's not Masterpiece Theater
on public television but a narrator with black-and-white
          footage, saying ". . . and then Miss Anderson,"

* * *

whereupon I blurt the words, *Marian* Anderson,

not sure why, and my wife, now silent,
which I take means to her, sure, it's 1939; who else?—
snubbed by the DAR, and some guy
named Walter White gets the Roosevelts to pull strings

so in April, out she walks
with the big Mr. Lincoln behind her, and I admit,
I really respect the fur coat; my wife's
not making a sound because we've joined

the 75,000 all dressed up, even the kids—
not a flip flop or midriff—when
Miss Anderson closes her eyes and sings,
"My country tis of thee."

It is eighty-something years later, when the words
"to thee I sing" become for her
"to thee we sing," which you might know,
is the song from now on,

we can't hear in any way but hers, whereupon
my wife turns to me, so I see
in her eyes why she—I mean everyone—
and I stopped breathing.

## TALK IN CHURCH

My wife can feel her horse moving
beneath her when she lies in bed at night
for two or three days after a ride, even
if a canter in the big shed with other moms,
which is solely an assumption of the body,
the hair of the flesh and bones that shake.
A Missouri Fox Trotter carries her down.

This convinces me of the presence of angels
for a moment, as when I stood on a boat,
believing a hand would hold us there
in the Grand Canal, overloaded with tourists,
so the large, lapping, stinking waves reached
the gunwales; the grumbling engine shooshed
and cajoled out of us all a confession.

Conversations with God should be private,
I was taught, so we bow our heads, bury
our faces, and whisper to a confessional grid
as if there were no earthly shadow behind
but a story, the one I overhear in church:
A woman says, "I should get off those pills,"
and her friend says, "I used to take too many."

The church pianist, Harry, plays a little louder;
and the one woman says, "They cost so much,"
and her friend says, "They don't do anything."
This is thy body, I sing, on the feast of nativity
of the mother of the son of God. Get the body
of thy horse beneath all women again, I pray,
and let it chew up the pasture at a gallop.

## FEEDING CHICKENS

No potato skins,
no avocado skins.
Start with the obvious:
no rhubarb leaves
for them or us,
no meat or dairy
for them, but yes,
crushed tomatoes
on linguine for us
and red blends
if content tends
to drift, and yes
to grit in your teeth
from farm work,
a pickup following
a pickup too close,
dually dust
on lilac leaves
and grass, discs
turning the fields,
windows sealed
dead of summer,
and across the yard
of things good,
scattered brown
lettuce, apple
peels from the pie.

## EVANS

The way it was in the nineties you stopped
on our walks to open a squeeze
coin purse and dispense quarters
to the homeless guys, sometimes dollars
for cigars, and sometimes we'd go

buy dinner for a crippled or wounded
vet without the company of a woman;
this, I add, was San Francisco, and now,
I carry my own red, plastic squeeze purse
back in the middle of the Middle West, a city

not to be flown over, where the raised-up
on-a-platform clerks at the convenience
store pause to watch me squeeze out
exactly the needed quarter and a penny,
say, relieving them—slowing down

the world's count a sec—so thank one
of San Francisco's best and native poets,
a guy named George, because we walked
everywhere or took a train, so always
there were stranded men and women

from the Basque or Italian, or Mission
(but for some reason not the Chinese)
parts of town, back when my landlady
on the second floor of Columbus Avenue
just down from Caffé Puccini and across

from a bar with an opera jukebox—her
gauzy curtains expanding in the windows
of our rooms—cooked neckbones when
$12 would get you a clean room and
you could walk downhill to the bookstore,

and the quarters loaded in your plastic
squeeze purse weighed like a lucky stone
in your leg pocket, so you could offer
amends to the lady in her flowered dress—
one of many reasons I think driving is a crime.

## LATE FOR MASS

Quick stepping through the parking lot
a June morning, sweating for the repose
of a soul yet-to-be-known,
and for Father Steve, may he be
refreshed on his travels—but to where
is not for the late to learn.

The substitute priest looks up
from his missal for the arrival,
himself, to push open the tall,
wooden, carved, portals of acclamation—
*Although you have hidden these things*

*from the wise and learned*—right
in the penitent's face, refreshingly,
for the soul does not repose
but wears a shirt ironed that morning
and stands on the pew, singing,
*My yoke is easy, and my burden light.*

## THE CHAIRS

The technician placed the chairs
on a sheet of glass when I challenged
the evenness of the legs, there

in the back room where he had
stored them for pick up.
He said the floor was uneven,

but so what? I wanted chairs
that sit solidly on any surface,
a Roman road or side street,

as I know women in Sicily
take their wooden chairs out
to the street to visit with friends,

or when I was a kid, our folks would
carry the steel-tubed kitchen chairs
with vinyl seats into the backyard,

where my aunts and girl cousins,
and very own dad, in fresh overalls,
and my Uncle Joe, God bless him,

and the McCarthys next door,
God knows who else, dragged
lawn chairs and stools, getting

the dog to move, and forming
a circle in the evening, solid
as my great aunt Sanina, sitting

on the wooden bench, her legs
beneath a flowered dress spread,
which is how I imagine she

steadied herself for the crossing:
Palermo to Naples, New York,
Chicago and down to St. Louis.

So I ordered these four, solid-teak
chairs when I got my own place,
and I wanted them not to move.

## FOR MARY FRANCES

*—after Issa*

Only four weeks old and already
your right arm is thinner
than your left; I should show you
the smallest animals on earth
to make you feel strong.

There's plenty an uncle might
tell you about your eyes
or German philosophers who said
the purpose of religion
is to adjust us to the inevitable.

But I waited, too, out here
while you grew up inside
your mother, doing fine,
and the first time one of us got
our hands on you, tore the tissue.

So, we learn to heal, as you do,
while one side stays small,
slung inside a scarf like a snail.
I just want you to know,
only four weeks old,

all of us will wonder how
we could have gone on without you.
After all, even a snail can climb
a mountain: but slowly, slowly,
as the perfect-minded and the pure.

# CODA

*Energy is eternal delight.*
—William Blake

## Acknowledgments

I would like to thank the editors and staffs of the following journals, collections, and anthologies where some of the poems in this book first appeared:

*Image*: "Squeezed In"
*Miramar*: "Arrivals," "Possum, Upon the Back Fence," "His Head"
*River Styx*: "The Sledge"
*New Letters*: "Virtuous Pigeons," "In the Back Pews on Easter . . ."
*Salt*: "Stopping in the Road for a Turtle," "Tasks Done and Undone," "Evans"
*Midwest Quarterly*: "Lights Out"
*North American Review*: "The Note," "The Day Marian Anderson Sings 'My Country 'Tis of Thee'"
*I-70 Review*: "Wishes for the World," "We Have Our Coats on," "Home Early," "Where I Was Then."
*Cloudbank*: "Feeding Chickens," "The Script"
*Tar River Poetry*: "Digging Sparky's Grave"
*Cottonwood*: "Account for This"
*Bridge Eight*: "They Shot Governor George," "Names of the Wives," "Dog in Church," "Lineation"
*Poetry International*: "Runner, Pausing, Alone"
*Bards Against Hunger* (anthology): "My Time"
*Curating Home* (anthology): "The Chairs"
*The Shining Years* (anthology): "Lineation."
*Kansas City Outloud II* (anthology): "For Mary Frances"
*Chickenhood* (Woods Colt Press chapbook): "Chickens Known & Unknown."
*Celebrating Thomas E. Kennedy* (anthology): "The Great Drying Off of the Women.

Additional gratitude goes to my dear friends, fellow poets and artists, mentors and guides. I mention two here: Judy Ray & David Ray, whose advice and examples continue to be inspirations.

## About the Author

Robert Stewart was born and raised in St. Louis, Missouri, served in the U.S. Navy, worked as an apprentice plumber, ditch digger and sewer worker, attended numerous colleges, and wound up with a career as an editor, writer, and sometimes teacher. His previous books include *Working Class: Poems* (Stephen F. Austin State University, 2018), *The Narrow Gate: Writing, Art, & Values* (essays, Serving House Books, 2014); *Outside Language: Essays* (Helicon Nine Editions, finalist for the PEN Center USA Literary Awards, 2004, and winner of the Thorpe Menn Award); *Plumbers* (poems, BkMk Press, revised second edition, 2017), and others. Chapbooks and monographs include the extended essay *On Swerving: The Way of William Stafford* (Literary House Press, 2007) and *Chickenhood* (seven poems about chickens, 2015).

He won a National Magazine Award for editing, from the American Society of Magazine Editors, the magazine industry's highest honor, for his work as editor of *New Letters* magazine, which he edited for eighteen years, until March 2020. He is the former director of *New Letters on the Air*, a nationally syndicated public-radio series, and BkMk Press, both formerly at the University of Missouri-Kansas City. He founded Midwest Poets Series in 1983 and directed the reading series for thirty-six years, on behalf of Rockhurst University in Kansas City.

His poems have appeared in *The Iowa Review, Image Journal, Poetry Northwest, I-70 Review, Prairie Schooner, Salt, Stand, Literary Review*, and other magazines. Anthology editorships include *Spud Songs: An Anthology of Potato Poems*, *Voices from the Interior: Missouri Poets*, *New American Essays*, and *Decade: Modern American Poets*. Robert Stewart's essays have appeared in *The Missouri Review, North American Review, Montreal Review, Italian Americana, KCStudio* and elsewhere. Feature articles have appeared in *Ingram's, The Kansas City Star, The New Art Examiner*, and others.

Made in the USA
Monee, IL
17 September 2024